SCARLATTI

SONATAS FOR THE KEYBOARD

EDITED BY MAURICE HINSON

Second Edition

*Cover art: Portrait of Maria Barbara, Queen of Spain.
A onetime student of Scarlatti, it was Maria Barbara for whom he wrote most of his harpsichord sonatas.*

This volume is dedicated to Dr. Willard Palmer,
with much admiration and appreciation.
Maurice Hinson

Contents

Foreword 4
Guide to Performance Practice in the Scarlatti Sonatas 5
Dynamics 5
Expressive Character 5
Fingering 5
Ornamentation 6
Other Ornaments and Performance Directions in Scarlatti's Sonatas 13
Phrasing and Articulation 14
Rhythmic Freedom in Scarlatti's Notation 15
Tempo 16
Playing Scarlatti on the Piano 16
The Influence of Spanish Folk Music and Dance on Scarlatti 17
Scarlatti's Pairing of the Sonatas 18
About This Edition 18
About Each Sonata 19
For Further Reading 21
Sonata in C Minor, K. 11 (L. 352) 22
Sonata in A Minor, K. 54 (L. 241) 24
Sonata in D Minor, K. 64 (L. 58) 28
Sonata in A Minor, K. 148 (L. 64) 30
Sonata in A Minor, K. 149 (L. 93) 32
Sonata in A Major, K. 208 (L. 238) 34
Sonata in A Major, K. 209 (L. 428) 36
Sonata in F Major, K. 274 (L. 297) 40
Sonata in E Minor, K. 291 (L. 61) 43
Sonata in F Major, K. 275 (L. 328) 46
Sonata in C Minor, K. 302 (L. 7) 50
Sonata in E Major, K. 380 (L. 23) 55
Sonata in C Major, K. 421 (L. 252) 58
Sonata in D Major, K. 430 (L. 463) 62

Foreword

Domenico Scarlatti (1685–1757) will be remembered as one of the most original composers of his century, and his music has maintained a foothold in the repertoire of today's pianists. His reputation stems primarily from his approximately 600 harpsichord sonatas written for his young student Princess Maria Barbara, who eventually became Queen of Spain. These sonatas have been preserved in large collections in important European libraries in Venice, Paris, Münster and Vienna.

Scarlatti's earliest collection of keyboard works (30) was published in 1738 under the title *Essercizi per Gravicembalo.* From this time on Scarlatti composed only harpsichord sonatas. He poured into these binary-form pieces an enormous variety and expressive range that has never been surpassed. His harpsichord style reflects an unfailing instinct for instrumental sonority as well as a desire for order and a matchless virtuoso flair. His music supports the fact that he was an irrepressible improviser, very closely bound with his instrument and not terribly interested in theoretical pursuits.

Scarlatti left only a few manuscript collections of sonatas when he died in Madrid on July 23, 1757. These remained almost unknown to the musical world until Carl Czerny, in 1839, published 200 of them in an edition in Vienna. This edition probably did more than anything else to keep Scarlatti's name alive during the 19th century, although Franz Liszt did perform some Scarlatti in his public recitals and was perhaps the first pianist to do so. A complete edition (11 volumes) was brought out by Alessandro Longo (1864–1945) in 1906–1908. Although this was a major contribution at the time, Longo edited the music through the eyes of a 19th-century Italian pianist and composer, and grouped the sonatas into arbitrarily arranged suites. He later added a supplement that included 45 sonatas.

It was left to the American harpsichordist Ralph Kirkpatrick (1911–1984) to write the definitive book on Scarlatti and to recatalog the sonatas according to a possible chronological order. The 555 sonatas are cataloged in his book *Domenico Scarlatti*, published originally in 1953. Kirkpatrick (K.), Longo (L.) and Longo Supplement (L. S.) numbers are used for identification purposes in these two volumes.

Title page of Scarlatti's original edition of *Essercizi per Gravicembalo* (1738).

Dynamics

Scarlatti left only a few rudimentary echo dynamics marked in sonatas K. 70, 73 and 88. The dynamic range available to him would have been that available on Spanish harpsichords of the period. These would have had essentially three colors: the sounds of the two keyboards alone plus the combination of the two. One keyboard would normally have had two stops at eight-foot pitch, with one of the stops voiced very delicately and the other voiced strongly. It appears that the majority of the late Scarlatti sonatas were composed for such an instrument as this.

Crescendos could be achieved by increasing the number of notes sounded closely together or by thickening the texture. This increased the dramatic intensity as well as the volume of a passage and thus can be found at climax points of the sonatas. (These points occur near the middle of each half of the sonata, not at the end of each half as might be expected.) The opposite effect occurs when textures are thinned; often Scarlatti has only two voices sounding together. Sometimes he uses thick chords or sudden bass notes for accent. Echo effects may be used but do so sparingly. Repeated phrases should be varied through changes in phrasing and touch as well as dynamics. Many of Scarlatti's sonatas incorporate the idea of orchestral solo-tutti alternation; the varied 18th-century orchestra contrasted with the solo part should be kept in mind in these pieces.

Expressive Character

These sonatas cover a broad expressive range, from the courtly to the savage, from an almost saccharin urbanity to a bitter violence. Their gaiety is made all the more intense by an undertone of tragedy. Their moments of meditative melancholy are at times overwhelmed by a surge of extroverted, operatic passion. In particular, Scarlatti has expressed in these works that part of his life that was lived in Spain.

Every mood and temperament seems to be spanned in these pieces, although most of them tend to display a single expressive character. If the performer can discern this character at the outset of learning a sonata, many problems will be solved almost automatically, particularly that of tempo. We can hear fanfare figures reminiscent of royal celebrations, and the guitar seems to have inspired gentle arpeggio strumming effects, internal pedal points, and percussive acciaccaturas. We are perhaps tempted to think that Scarlatti played the guitar, but there is no evidence to support this notion. He simply heard that instrument and was inspired by its possibilities and versatility.

Fingering

Correct employment of the fingers is inseparably related to the whole art of performance. C. P. E. Bach

1. Good fingering involves using as little motion as necessary to project the musical content and ensure security.
2. Scarlatti gives specific fingering directions for unusual situations. *Mutandi i deti* means "change the fingers."

Sonata in D Major, K. 96 (L. 465), measure 33

Con dedo solo means "with one finger" (i.e., glissando).

Sonata in F Major, K. 379 (L. 73), measure 33

These directions are clearly to make the hand's behavior more acrobatic and less orthodox.

3. Scarlatti's only other fingering indications are restricted to directions for distributing the music between the hands (*L* for left hand, *R* for right hand) or for changing fingers on long trills.
4. Tempo must be considered when working out fingering. What will work at a slow tempo may not work at a fast tempo.
5. Try hands alone when fingering a fast passage—up to tempo.
6. Difficult fingerings can often be more easily solved by working backwards from a place in the music where the fingering is easy to determine.
7. Select fingering that agrees as much as possible with the music's articulation and phrasing.
8. Sudden hand shifts can produce certain articulation effects, as the next example shows:

Sonata in A Minor, K. 175 (L. 429), measures 1–4

9. Do not write in fingerings indiscriminately. This is sometimes a crutch and often a waste of time. Write in only the essential fingerings for technical and expressive requirements. The editor has indicated only what he considers to be essential fingering.

Ornamentation

Scarlatti, as well as his contemporary, J. S. Bach, usually wrote out the actual notes of his ornaments. Scarlatti did not leave any tables or explanatory directions for ornaments. Some authorities feel that, except for the addition of an occasional appoggiatura or trill, Scarlatti did not expect the performer to add many florid embellishments as was the norm for most Italian singers and violinists when performing music of their time. Fortunately for us, C. P. E. Bach, in his treatise *Essay on the True Art of Playing Keyboard Instruments*, dealt with most of the ornamentation problems found in Scarlatti's music.

The Appoggiatura: The appoggiatura appears in music as a small note tied to a normal-sized note and is commonly called a grace note today. Appoggiatura comes from the Italian word *appoggiare*, to lean or rest, and is thus a note that seems to lean on the note that follows it. The appoggiatura is an accented dissonance and should be played on the beat, taking its value from the note that follows. The value of this main note and its context, not the appoggiatura's notation, determine the length of the appoggiatura. Scarlatti uses all of the following to indicate appoggiaturas:

The appoggiatura should be slurred quietly to the main note, whether indicated or not.

Long Appoggiatura: This is the most frequently used form; it takes half the time value of its main note.

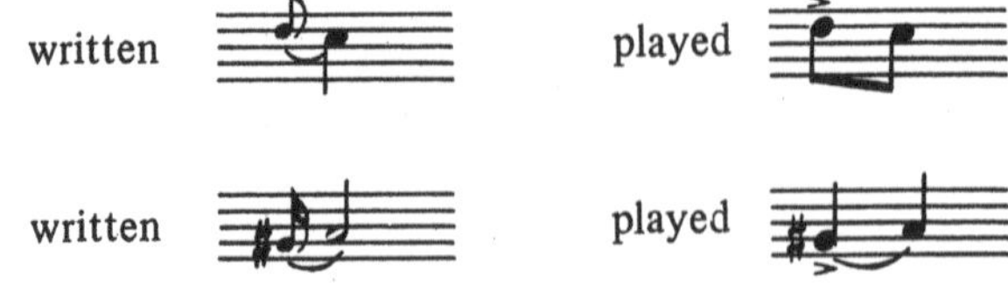

Long appoggiaturas may take two-thirds of the value of the main note if this note is dotted (more easily divisible by three).

Short Appoggiatura: Short appoggiaturas take as little time as possible from the main note. They frequently occur before fast notes and must be played with great rapidity so the main rhythmic outline remains intact.

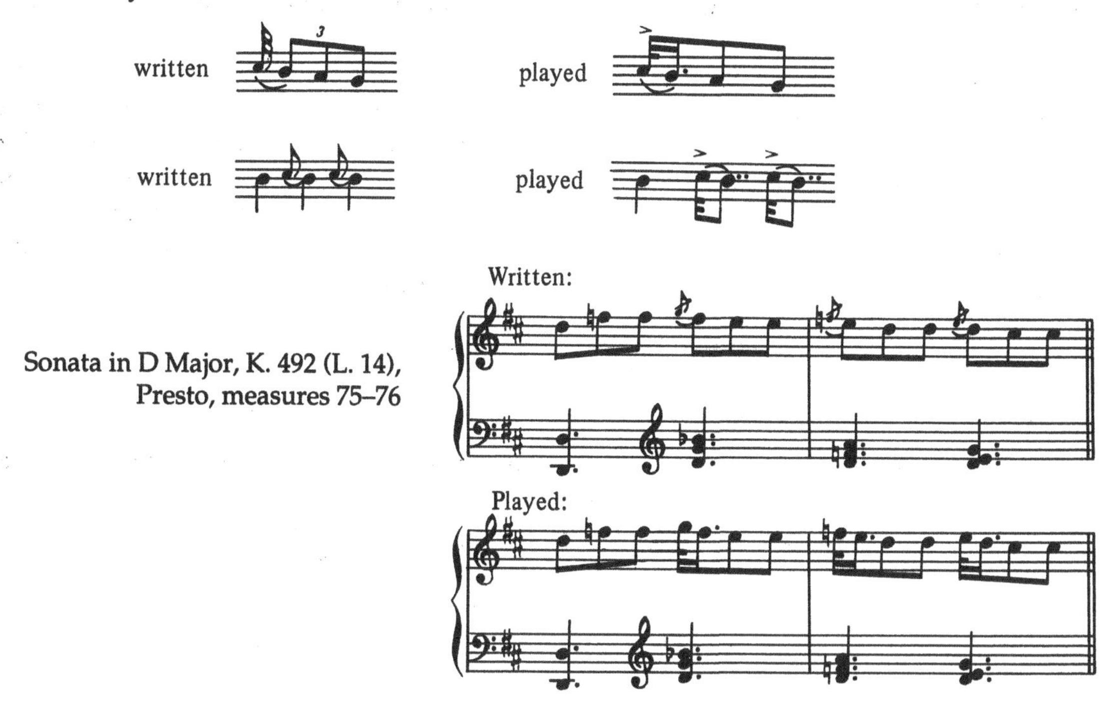

Occasionally Scarlatti is inconsistent with his notation and in parallel passages realizes the appoggiaturas (i.e., writes them out), thereby giving us clues as to how they should be performed.

Sonata in B Major, K. 261 (L. 148), Allegro

Sonata in E Major, K. 531 (L. 430), Allegro

Occasionally groups of grace notes should be played before the beat when the physical layout of the keyboard and/or musical logic seem to suggest this realization.

Sonata in G Minor, K. 8 (L. 488), Allegro

The Slide (Schleifer): Scarlatti writes this out using two, three or four small notes. It may begin below or above its main note. It should be played on the beat gracefully and quickly.

written played

Sonata in E Major, K. 495 (L. 426), Allegro, measure 53

The Trill: Scarlatti uses trill signs ***w***, *tr*, and *trw* interchangeably. They give no indication regarding the kind of trill to be played, its length or its speed. Scarlatti's trills begin (almost without exception) on the same beat of the main (written) note and usually on the upper auxiliary (the note above the main note). They should contain at least four notes, with the performer deciding on the speed and duration of the trill and whether terminating notes should be added. The final note should be the trill's main note.

Sonata in B-flat Major, K. 442 (L. 319), Allegro, measure 1

Sonata in G Major, K. 425 (L. 333), Allegro molto, measures 82–85

Trills with Termination (Suffix) or Finishing Notes: Scarlatti sometimes indicates a termination or ending to a trill in normal-sized notes. These terminating or finishing notes should be played at the same speed as the trill, thereby fusing with the body of the trill. The terminated trill requires at least six notes. The performer may add a termination consisting of the lower auxiliary and main note to any trill that is followed by the next higher or lower scale note.

Sonata in F Major, K. 540 (L. S. 17), Allegretto, measures 18–20

Scarlatti will sometimes add more than two terminating notes to make the connection smooth with the following main note.

Sonata in F Minor, K. 183 (L. 473), Allegro, measures 20–21

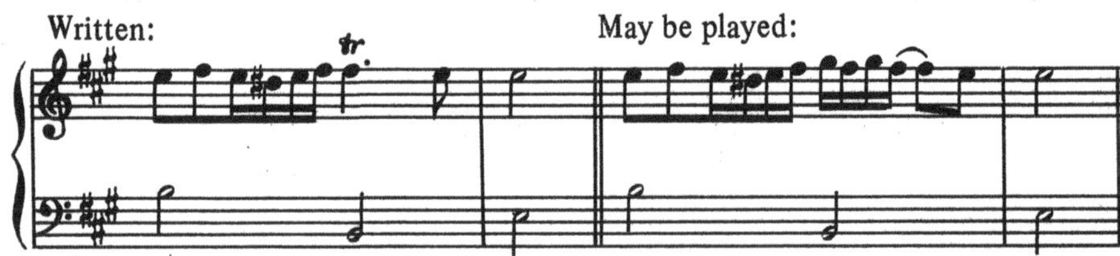

Chains of moving trills intended to sound like a melodic line sound more musical with terminating notes.

Sonata in C Major, K. 501 (L. 137), Allegretto, measures 51–52

A termination which anticipates the next note may be added to a trill. Let the trill come to a stop before its full time value, pause very briefly, and then play the following note quickly in anticipation of the next note.

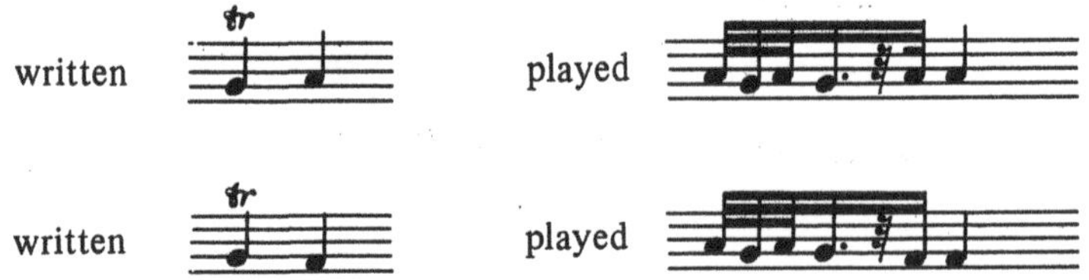

Scarlatti frequently follows the last note of a trill with an appoggiatura.

Sonata in F Major, K. 256 (L. 228), Andante, measures 8–9

Generally, the performer should not add terminating trill notes when the trill is followed by a rest, a double bar or a main note that is further away than the next stepwise scale tone.

Tied Trill: Scarlatti uses this ornament infrequently; it consists of a trill which is preceded by the same note as its upper auxiliary. Do not repeat the beginning note of the trill, but instead tie the preceding note to the first note of the trill. A slur extends from the preceding note to the trill, which is the determining factor in the notation.

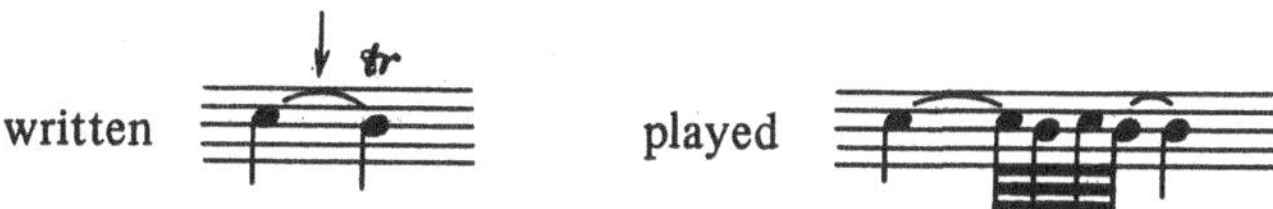

Do not interpret this slur (indicated by an arrow) as being only an indication of legato; it is much more than that. This ornament sounds the most musical when incorporated into a smooth diatonic line where no accent is necessary.

Sonata in G Major, K. 412 (L. 182), Allegro, measure 35

Sometimes Scarlatti will write an appoggiatura which repeats the previous note, mainly as a precaution against using a tied trill.

Sonata in E Minor, K. 291 (L. 61), Andante, measures 15–16

Trill Substitutes on Quick Notes: If the performer cannot play the full four notes for a trill on a quick note, an upper appoggiatura may be substituted in its place.

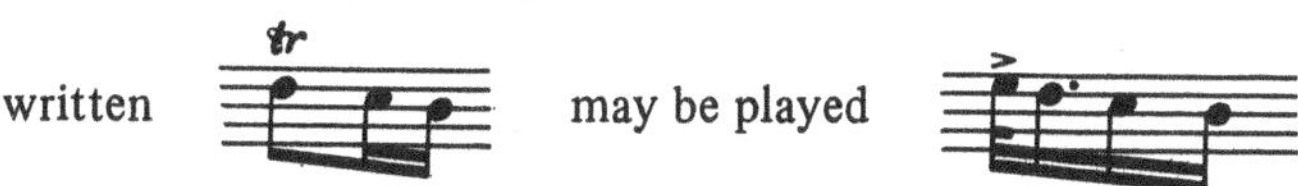

Sonata in F Major, K. 349 (L. 170), Allegro, measures 108–109

Written:

Played:

Trill Preceded by an Upper Appoggiatura: When Scarlatti uses a small note preceding a trill, this indicates an appoggiatura from above. This emphasizes the appoggiatura function of the upper trill note.

Sonata in E Major, K. 206 (L. 257), Andante, measures 6–7

Written: Played:

Lower Appoggiatura and Trill: This generally should be interpreted as a long appoggiatura from below followed by an unprepared trill. This is one situation where the trill begins on the main note.

Sonata in C Major, K. 527 (L. 458), Allegro assai, measures 11–12

Written: Played:

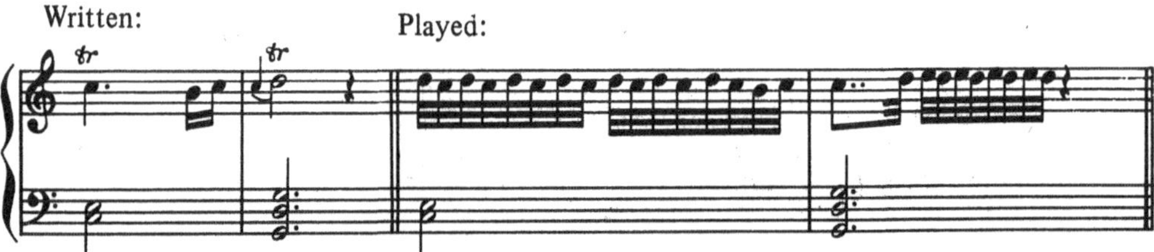

Trill with Prefix: Small notes before a trill indicate the trill with prefix. The small notes should be played on the beat. Their speed is determined by the context of the trill.

Sonata in F Major, K. 256 (L. 228), Andante, measures 21–22

Written: Played:

Sonata in B-flat Major, K. 489 (L. S. 41), Allegro, measure 95

Written: Played:

Tremulo: Scarlatti uses the word *Tremulo* or its abbreviation *Tre., Trem*[lo], or *Trem* in some of the sonatas. It appears to mean the same thing as a trill.

Double Trill: When a double trill is indicated in one hand, no terminating notes should be added.

Sonata in F Major, K. 541 (L. 120), Allegretto, measure 61

Other Ornaments and Performance Directions in Scarlatti's Sonatas

Mordent: Scarlatti writes out this ornament in normal-sized notation. He does not use the conventional sign ⁂.

Turn: Scarlatti writes out the turn, usually in small notes, rather than using the ∾ sign.

Sonata in D Major, K. 490 (L. 206), Cantabile, measure 26

Arpeggiation of Chords: Scarlatti did not use an arpeggio sign to indicate when a chord should be broken. But the rolling of chords either upwards or downwards, from the top or bottom towards the middle, etc., was an expressive device frequently used in Baroque keyboard music. Scarlatti surely had arpeggio usage in mind in the following example (small notes *on the beat*, not before it):

Sonata in E Minor, K. 394 (L. 275), Allegro, measure 64

Since both fast and slow arpeggiated chords are such an essential part of harpsichord technique, there is no doubt that Scarlatti used them frequently.

Acciaccatura: This word means "crushing" and refers to an auxiliary note struck simultaneously with its resolution. Scarlatti never indicated the use of an acciaccatura in his sonatas by a sign, but rather included them in chords as nonharmonic dissonances. In fact, this is one of the most distinctive features of Scarlatti's style. He clearly relishes these discords for their percussive effect, and these note clusters can be best explained, perhaps, by analogy with guitar music.

Sonata in A Minor, K. 175 (L. 429), Allegro, measures 1–3

The violent discords of K. 490 sound wonderful on the harpsichord and should not be played more quietly on the piano—but the thicker sound of the piano could be thinned by playing the chords as quick arpeggios and releasing some of the keys like:

Sonata in D Major, K. 490 (L. 206), measure 35

Adding Ornaments: Numerous situations in these sonatas suggest the addition of ornaments, especially on repeats. Add them at the following places:

1. When a strong dominant-tonic progression takes place, usually at the end of a large section.

Sonata in B-flat Major, K. 393 (L. 74), Minuet, measures 33–34

2. When a dotted pattern occurs at a cadence, such as a dotted quarter followed by an eighth, a trill can be interpolated. The short note (eighth) should be made even shorter.

Sonata in D Minor, K. 89b (L. 211), Grave, measures 17–19

Ornaments are missing sometimes when consistency would lead the performer to expect them. In such places, the performer must decide whether to insert them or whether there is perhaps some reason for the omission.

Phrasing and Articulation

Scarlatti left few phrasing marks, slurs or staccato indications in the sonatas. But frequently he uses only a few slurs to indicate a pattern which is to be continued. Notes that form a broken chord with slurs over or under it indicate the keys are to be held down and sounded as a chord.

Smaller patterns underlie much of Scarlatti's figuration, and the performer must be aware of their importance. Stepwise movement tends to be more connected (legato) while skips tend to be more distinctly articulated (staccato). The normal touch for pieces in a fast or moderate tempo was the "ordinary movement," which meant a slight detaching of the notes that was proportionate to their time values. This is an excellent device for producing clarity. Slower movements used more sustained notes.

Small breaths of articulated silence should normally be made before all appoggiaturas, before wide skips, before long tied notes and often before a change in prevailing note values in a passage.

C. P. E. Bach in his *Essay* gives a clue as how to arrive at correct phrasing: "above all, lose no opportunity to hear accomplished singing. Indeed, it is a good practice to sing instrumental melodies, so as to be able to reach an understanding of their correct performance." The human voice is the natural medium of musical expression. Vocal phrases are supported by a single breath, and phrase divisions are set off by breath intake. In Scarlatti's keyboard music there are breathing places as there are in song and speech, and the sensitive pianist can bring vitality and expressiveness to the music by imitating singers just as C. P. E. Bach suggested. Scarlatti's music tends to use more upbeat phrasing than on-the-beat phrasing. Dance gestures or vocal style underlie most of Scarlatti's musical phrasing.

Rhythmic Freedom in Scarlatti's Notation

Scarlatti's rhythmic treatment reflected the performance practice of his time, when much more was left to the performer's discretion than today. Certain alterations and unwritten freedoms were taken for granted.

Dotted Rhythms: Short notes following dotted notes were shorter than notated. This "overdotting" adds a strongly projected rhythm and is used by Scarlatti in a number of his sonatas.

Sonata in F Minor, K. 364 (L. 436), Allegro, measures 77–78

A rhythmic pattern written as:

was often altered to be performed like:

Sonata in F Minor, K. 238 (L. 27), Andante, measure 40

Triplet Rhythms: Where triplet rhythm predominates, notated pairs of eighths should be adjusted to fit the triplet pattern. Notice the following example where the "overdotted" trill should be adjusted to fit the triplet pattern. To clarify the rhythm, the trill should be stopped on the dot.

Sonata in G Major, K. 391 (L. 79), Allegro, measures 34–36

When Scarlatti uses the word *Arbitri,* he means for the passage to be played somewhat freely.

Tempo

Scarlatti left Italian terms like "allegro," "presto" or "andante," etc., at the beginning of his sonatas, but unfortunately these words do not tell us much about tempo. They serve more to indicate rhythmic character, context and mood. Most of us play Scarlatti too fast. A "presto" with Scarlatti may be more accurately interpreted as "alert and lively" than as a license for a virtuosic display of dexterity. Even though Scarlatti was a spectacular virtuoso, his keyboard technique, as reflected in these sonatas, must always be counterbalanced by considerations of harmonic nuance, vocal line, and sharp rhythmic detail that should be reflected in the performer's choice of tempo.

Remember, a fast tempo sounds even faster to the listener than to the performer. All great music surely can be performed expressively at more than one tempo. Many of Scarlatti's sonatas require more than one rate of speed, especially the ones containing contrasting sections.

Some of the sonatas are dance movements, and considerable tempo guidance can be derived from a basic knowledge of what these dances were and how they moved. The section *About Each Sonata* provides some assistance in this area.

Ornamentation often provides insights regarding tempo. Ornaments that sound strident, bumpy and forced into the musical texture are often an indication that the natural movement of the sonata is too fast.

The performer must decide on a tempo that permits clarity in the melodic figuration and harmonic changes. The editorial suggested metronome marks are just that: suggestions. Each performer must ultimately select a tempo suggested by the music that will allow him/her best to realize the mood and character of the music.

Playing Scarlatti on the Piano

The pianist should not attempt to imitate a harpsichord. He/she should not try to use all the resources of the piano, for that could destroy the character of the music, but rather should use the piano coloristically and with much imagination. Ralph Kirkpatrick says it best in his monumental book on Scarlatti:

> Nothing is more fatal than allowing the musical imagination to be restricted by the limits of two or three colors or by the limitations of any instrument one is using . . . Scarlatti's harpsichord music is full of effects of color conceived in extra-harpsichord terms. The player of Scarlatti, no matter what the restrictions of his instrument, must be ready at all times to think in terms of imaginary orchestration, of the voice, of the sounds concomitant with the Spanish dance, of the not-strictly musical or of the frankly extra-musical sound effects of which I have spoken in connection with the real-life stimulus that lies, barely concealed or transformed almost beyond recognition, behind so much of Scarlatti's music. Scarlatti's harpsichord, while supremely itself, is continually menacing a transformation into something else. It can never be taken literally.

If the reader has heard Vladimir Horowitz perform Scarlatti, then he/she has some idea of the amazing possibilities that are available when playing Scarlatti on our wonderful instrument, the piano. Indeed, Scarlatti's work has come to be considered the lawful property of the pianist, as well as, of course, the harpsichordist.

These sonatas present a physical challenge to the pianist, who must train his/her hands to move rapidly over the keyboard and his/her fingers to dance nimbly "on the spot" (for fast repeated notes).

Although not present on Scarlatti's harpsichord, the damper pedal can be used for adding color. But it should not be used in a way that would cause muddiness or detract from the clarity of the writing. Learn the sonatas first without pedal, then add pedaling for occasional accents or shadings of nuance. The una corda (soft or left) pedal may be used to change tone color, as well as to play quietly.

Pianists with special feeling for specific musical values, for line, rhythm and tapestrylike harmonic texture, will succeed in making these sonatas sound best on the piano, even if they have only slight acquaintance with the harpsichord.

The Influence of Spanish Folk Music and Dance on Scarlatti

The study of Spanish folk music and dance is very helpful in understanding Scarlatti's sonatas. Domenico left Italy at the age of 36 and spent the rest of his life on the Iberian peninsula. He heard folk music and saw folk dancing in Seville, Cadiz, Granada and major cities in the province of Andalusia. Charles Burney, the well-known historian, said: "Scarlatti imitated the melody of tunes sung by carriers, mutineers and common people." It is fairly easy for anyone with some knowledge of Spanish folk music and dance to feel the spirit of this music in Scarlatti, but it is difficult to try to define it. One musician who thoroughly understood the Spanish element in Scarlatti was Manuel de Falla (1876–1946), himself a native of Cadiz and an authority on the music of Andalusia. He believed that Scarlatti could be considered the classic Spanish composer. De Falla also felt that Scarlatti understood Spanish harmony as it is found in the guitar music of Andalusia. These harmonic techniques are called flamenco, where both strumming and passagework are featured in guitar playing for the dance. The similarities between many of these sonatas and the genuine folk flamenco as Scarlatti knew it, are surprising.

Andalusian folk music uses the Phrygian mode, but with an important modification—a raised third. In the Phrygian mode of the key of C major, this would result in: E, F, G-sharp, A, B, C, D, E. Much of the Andalusian music hovers between G-sharp and G-natural, and Scarlatti used this characteristic and the harmonies associated with it in many of his Spanish-sounding passages.

The sonata K. 490 (see pages 38–41 in Vol. II) is a *saeta*. The *saeta* is a form of *cante* (singing) improvised in Seville's streets during Holy Week processions as a demonstration of popular religious feeling. An accompanying drum plays this somber, marchlike rhythm:

with a poignant melody using the same rhythm. This *cante* form has hardly changed since about 1730. Scarlatti left Seville in 1733 and never returned to Andalusia. This would probably date this sonata from around the early 1730s.

Long sections of K. 492 (see pages 42–45 in Vol. II) are very similar to the *bulerias*, a dance full of vivacious rhythmic insistence. The *bulerias* is one of the most joyful of the flamenco dances (a dance style mainly associated with the Gypsies of Andalusia). Sonata K. 421 (see pages 58–61 in Vol. I) contains chromatic passages found in many flamenco pieces. Sonata K. 502 (see pages 46–49 in Vol. II) has unmistakable characteristics of a lively *peteneras* (a flamenco form of Andalusian origin that is both danced and sung). Sonata K. 519 (pages 54–57 in Vol. II) is a fast dance in triplet time in the minor followed by a section in the major; this minor/major arrangement is characteristic of Andalusian music. Sonata K. 116 (pages 28–31 in Vol. II) is a typically spirited Andalusian piece.

There are numerous examples of the *canarios* (an old quick dance associated with the Canary Islands), the *fandango* (an old Spanish dance with strongly marked 3/4 rhythm) and the *seguidilla* (a highly popular Spanish dance and song in quick 3/4 tempo) in the sonatas. Scarlatti could have heard all of these dances in Seville. Sonata K. 105 (pages 24–27 in Vol. II) and K. 209 (pages 36–39 in Vol. I) are fine examples of the *jota*, a genre of song and dance with rapid, strong and energetic steps which is closely related to the *fandango*.

It appears that Scarlatti wrote many of these sonatas during his first four years in Spain, when he was under the strong influence of Andalusian music. This would seem to contradict Kirkpatrick's belief that the larger part of them were composed during the final five years of Scarlatti's life.

Scarlatti's sonatas, with their leaps, wide movements (e.g., hand crossings) and driving rhythms, seem to reflect the bodily freedom required of the dance. These works also contain traditional dances such as the *gavottes*, *gigas* and *minuets*, more like "concert versions" or "evocations" of the original dance forms, as well as numerous unidentified *boleros*, *sicilianos* and *tarantellas*. The sensitive performer should be aware of their underlying significance and the strong Spanish influence found in many of these sonatas.

Scarlatti's Pairing of the Sonatas

Scarlatti paired many of his sonatas. In fact, Kirkpatrick believes that most of the sonatas after K. 98 were conceived in this manner. However, conflicting views exist on this point, and since the sequence of sonatas varies greatly from source to source, the editor has included only three pairs of sonatas, K. 148 and 149, K. 208 and 209, and K. 274 and 275 (not consecutive for better page turns), in Vol. I. Yet contrasting two-movement sonatas were common in the 18th century, and some of the pieces are most attractive when performed in combination. However, if a student is better able to handle one sonata than the other, there is no reason why one can't be learned and played and the other postponed until later. Each sonata is an interesting piece in its own right. Scarlatti also made larger groupings than two sonatas.

About This Edition

The main purposes of this edition are to provide an introduction to performance practice in the Scarlatti sonatas, and to provide two volumes of some of these wonderfully rich and varied keyboard sonatas.

Performance practice refers to the knowledge of performance conventions, which enables a performer to create an intelligent performance. In the context of notated music, performance practice is usually thought to encompass everything about performance that is not clearly specified in notation. This edition can only introduce a few of the most important areas that must be considered in performing Scarlatti's sonatas: dynamics, expressive character, fingering, ornamentation, phrasing, rhythmic treatment and tempo.

Domenico Scarlatti
(1685–1757)
Lithograph by Alfred Lemoine

Today, over 200 years after his death, hundreds of Scarlatti's sonatas are still practically unknown. The sonatas in this edition have been selected primarily for the intermediate to moderately advanced student. Since many of Scarlatti's earlier *Essercizi* have appeared in collections and anthologies, this edition includes only one sonata from that collection plus some later, less familiar and familiar sonatas, with the Venice and Parma manuscript collections being used as the basis for the text.

This is a performing edition that includes suggested editorial additions such as dynamics, fingering, articulation and phrasing, realization of ornaments and metronome indications. Everything in parentheses is also editorial. Each sonata has been approached with the idea of presenting an easily readable, yet thoroughly edited score that would provide the less advanced student with a clear guide for a musical and stylistically correct performance.

The editor has retained all of Scarlatti's indications for distributions between the hands. Scarlatti's use of the letters M for manca (left hand) and D for destra (right hand) has been translated in the music to *L* and *R*.

This edition has been prepared for performing these works on the piano and this instrument is treated on its own terms, with full appreciation of its tonal resources. All of the expressive qualities of the harpsichord are utilized as effectively as possible. No pedal indications have been used in this edition but there is no reason pedal should not be used as a coloring device when performing these sonatas on the piano. See the section *Playing Scarlatti on the Piano,* page 16.

To assist the teacher and performer, four categories of grading (Early Intermediate, Intermediate, Late Intermediate and Early Advanced) are used that generally correspond to the accepted divisions of difficulty. No gradings can be absolute, and the assignment of a grade category does not mean that all pieces of the same category are equally interchangeable. A choice must be made according to the musical development, technical ability and maturity of the performer.

Historical information, performance problems and suggestions related to each sonata are discussed in the following section, *About Each Sonata*.

I wish to thank the staffs of the following libraries who helped me by replying to questions and supplying material: Convento San Francesco della Vigna, Venice; Diözesan-Bibliothek, Münster; and Real Conservatorio de Música, Madrid. To all of these, and to the several friends and colleagues who have shared their experience of Scarlatti's music with me, I extend my warmest thanks.

There is no better way of closing this section than to use Scarlatti's own words to his readers from the introduction to his *Essercizi*, published in 1738:

VIVI FELICE
(live happily).

About Each Sonata

Sonata in C Minor
K. 11 (L. 352) *Page 22*

A secure march feeling will help in the projection of this sonata. Let up slightly with dynamics on the hand-crossing sections. Delicate figuration abounds with trills tucked in here and there. Be especially careful of the clef changes, scalar patterns and arpeggios. This is the only sonata of the *Essercizi* (sonatas 1–30 published in England in 1738; the term *Essercizi* should be construed in much the same sense as the *Etudes* of Chopin) that has no character or tempo indication. This particular edition is marked Allegro (non troppo). All of the others are marked Allegro or Presto. Intermediate.

Sonata in A Minor
K. 54 (L. 241) *Page 24*

Scarlatti makes equal demands on the hands with respect to octave passages in this piece. It is based on a very active germinal rhythmic pattern. Do not let the tarantella eighths go too fast. The long sections of contrapuntal hand crossings are taxing, and any tempo over ♩ = c. 120 can cause major problems for many pianists. Think of two pulses per measure; this will add buoyancy and still let the chromatic motives be clearly heard. Late Intermediate.

Sonata in D Minor
K. 64 (L. 58) *Page 28*

This sonata is couched in strong homophonic sonorities. Left-hand chords support a delightful right-hand melody. Its straightforward rhythm encounters a few trills but no other ornaments. Cluster-like chords and wide stretches document Scarlatti's authentic harmonic style. Subtitled *Gavota*, its characteristics include four-measure construction and single motive with fanciful syncopation. Early Intermediate.

Sonata in A Minor
K. 148 (L. 64) *Page 30*

This basically two-voice sonata features appoggiaturas, trills and turns. The expressive lines should move freely and without strong accent. This type of writing is contrasted with more rhythmic sections at measures 17–24 and 73–79. The tied trill at measure 68 allows for a very smooth line. Early Intermediate.

Sonata in A Minor
K. 149 (L. 93) *Page 32*

K. 148 and 149 form a pair of sonatas and should be played together if possible. They provide strong contrast. K. 149 seems to display Spanish influence with its rhythmic treatment and repeated notes (guitar influence). The prevailing touch should be rather nonlegato with careful regard for phrasing. The sighlike motive (measures 3, 4, 10, 11, 17–19, etc.) should be very expressive: lift the hand quickly but quietly after playing each group. The repeated notes in measures 6–8, 12, 20–21, etc., should not be overly staccato, i.e., keep the fingers close to the surface of the keys. This pair of sonatas may have been written for the early fortepiano since they are quite different in character from Scarlatti's early harpsichord writing, and there were fortepianos present at the Spanish court. Early Intermediate.

Sonata in A Major
K. 208 (L. 238) *Page 34*

A simple chordal bass accompanies a lovely cantabile melody in a sustained tranquil mood. Syncopations move the melody, and the performer must be careful not to accent the melodic note of resolution. The articulation should basically be staccato for eighth notes and legato for 16ths. This sonata requires only a limited range of color: slight dynamic changes on the piano plus clear phrasing and articulation. A fine control of rhythmic freedom is also helpful here—for slight accelerandos at measures 11–13 and 16–24 and for stretching the tempo at measures 5–6 and 8–9. Kirkpatrick says this sonata:

> ...is courtly flamenco music, rendered elegant and suitable for the confines of the royal palace, as were its players and singers when Goya brought them into his tapestry cartoons a few years later.

(Kirkpatrick, 167). Early Intermediate.

Sonata in A Major
K. 209 (L. 428) *Page 36*

This is the companion piece for K. 208. K. 209 is a *jota* and entails a drastic change of mood from K. 208. Stamping heels, snapping castanets and flurrying feet are implied in this dance—especially in the crescendos of rhythmic acceleration that climax with the trills in measures 45 and 61. Take a little more time with these two measures. The orchestral principal of alternate solo and tutti is used here. A few Alberti figures occur plus 16th-note scalar figuration. This is surely one of Scarlatti's happiest sonatas, and the combination of K. 208 with 209 makes a wonderful recital grouping. Intermediate.

Sonata in F Major
K. 274 (L. 297) *Page 40*

This is the companion piece for K. 275. Both sections of this attractive sonata begin with imitation similar to a two-part invention. Versatile use of contrary motion, altered scales and echoing parallel thirds and sixths between the hands make for a most appealing piece. The horn call ideas in the left hand at measures 24–28 should be brought out slightly louder than the right-hand material. The left-hand part at measures 33–36 also should be heard over the right hand due to its thematic significance. Articulation of the figure ♫♩ (lifting the hand after the quarter) is of special importance for a successful performance of this sonata. Early Intermediate.

Sonata in E Minor
K. 291 (L. 61) *Page 43*

This sonata features a flutelike melody over a simple accompaniment. The thematic material uses a unifying rhythmic pattern that is frequently repeated, thereby making this piece easy to memorize. In performing this sonata, be sure that the notes not slurred are played distinctly nonlegato. Notice the different dynamic distinctions between the hands. Early Intermediate.

Sonata in F Major
K. 275 (L. 328) *Page 46*

Thematic material constantly expands throughout this sonata. The opening motive is thickened by adding a voice, rhythmic figuration contrasts with it, and finally it is distilled into shorter note values. All of these devices add tension that is released only in the final few measures. Technical devices include double thirds, sustained and moving notes, 16th-note scales and syncopation. The editor has added a trill at measure 45 to match a similar occurrence at measure 61. Intermediate.

Sonata in C Minor
K. 302 (L. 7) *Page 50*

This sonata is a study in triplets, with interesting modulations and varying treatment of the sequential ideas within the triplet pattern. Cadenzalike scales at measures 57–60 and 98–101 add excitement and intensity. The section from measure 62 to 85 contains some unsettled harmonic wandering with intricate progressions. This is counterbalanced by a strong C major tonality from measure 86 to the end. Therefore, in interpreting this sonata, the performer must be able to interpret the quick changes of temperament in the various sections like a fine actor. Intermediate.

Sonata in E Major
K. 380 (L. 23) *Page 55*

This stately sonata displays the elegance of a polonaise, with trumpet calls. It is based on two ideas: the open fifth and repeated use of two-note slurs. The open fifth is used in both the primary and secondary themes. The secondary theme of horn-call open fifths in a repeated rhythm imitated between the hands is especially unique. Some of the technical problems involve complex ornamentation, two-note slurs, 16th-note scalar figuration and syncopation. It is a pleasure to perform this most successful piece, which requires a delicate approach and clean technique. Early Advanced.

Sonata in C Major
K. 421 (L. 252) *Page 58*

This sonata is dominated largely by a repeated-note figure. It contains chromatic passages present in many flamenco pieces and requires digital independence. Measures 32–43 must not be strongly accented on the first beat since all three voices sound at that time, which already provides plenty of accent. Colorful dissonances are mixed with quick two-note repetitions that easily articulate themselves. Eighths should be separated. Intricate patterns develop from the wide-interval left-hand leaps. Numerous clef changes should keep the eyes alert. The addition of short trills at measures 66 and 142 is appropriate. Early Advanced.

Sonata in D Major
K. 430 (L. 463) *Page 62*

The opening indication tells the performer that this lively piece should be performed "not quite presto, but in the tempo of a ballet or dance." Therefore, the tempo of this dance should be sprightly, yet light and bouncy. It is obstinate in its dancing triple time. Quick jumps and leaps are challenging and trills and double notes require fast execution. The final measures (96 to the end) recall the echo of a hunting horn fading in the distance as the dancers leave the stage. The dancelike quality of this sonata has much audience appeal. Intermediate.

For Further Reading

Malcolm Boyd. *Domenico Scarlatti—Master of Music.* New York: Schirmer Books, 1986.

Jane Clark. "Domenico Scarlatti and Spanish Folk Music," *Early Music,* vol. 4 (1976):19–24.

Ralph Kirkpatrick. *Domenico Scarlatti.* Princeton University Press, 1953.

Carolyn Maxwell. *Scarlatti Solo Piano Literature.* Boulder: Maxwell Music Evaluation, 1985.

Sonata in C Minor

15
p
L
18
mf
f
mf
21
p
L
23
p
25
mf
27
p
pp

Sonata in A Minor

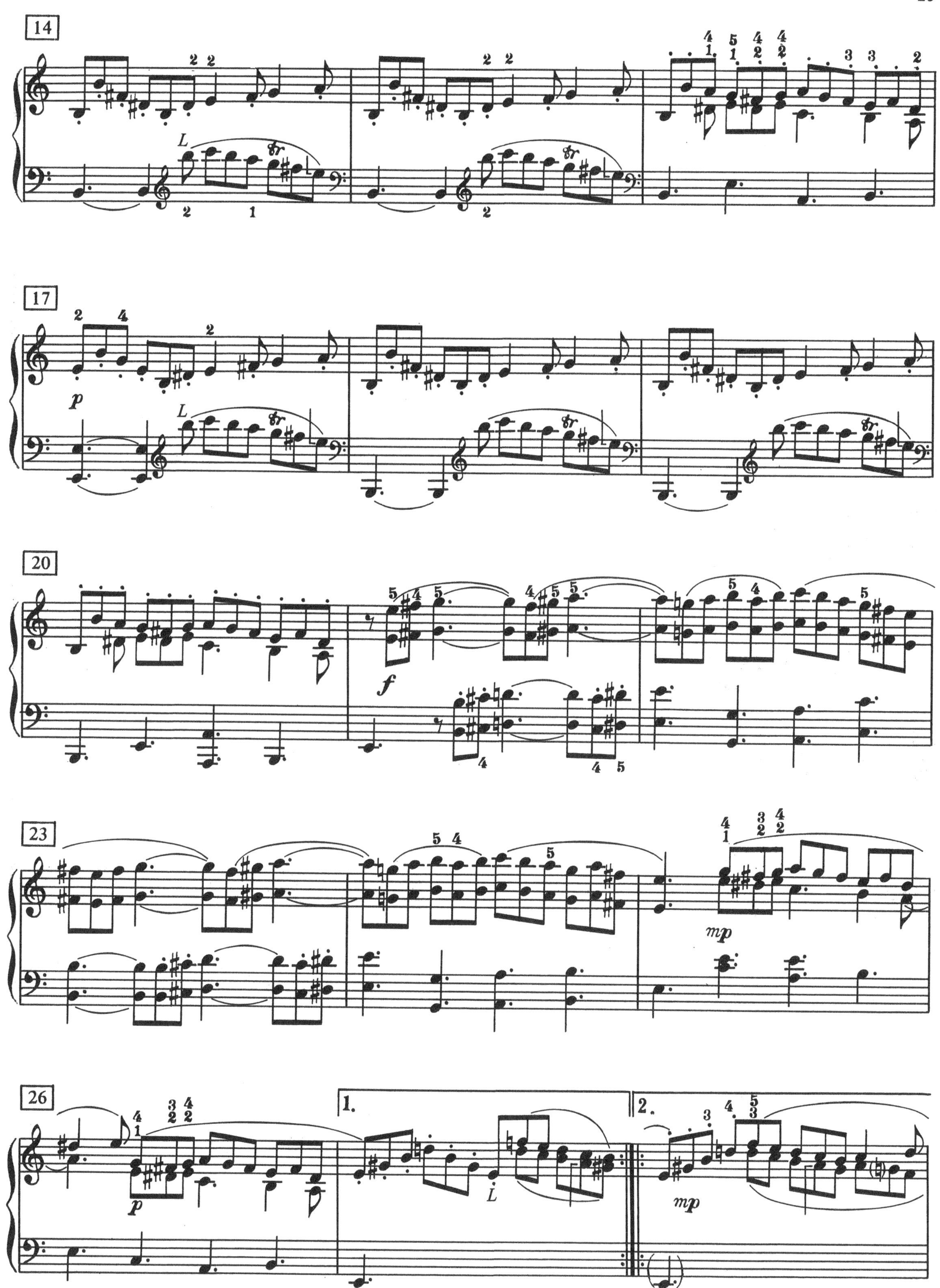

14
17
p
20
f
23
mp
26
p
1.
2.
mp

28
p
31
p
mp
34
p
mp
cresc.
37
40
mf

43
46
49
52
55
d
p
f
mp
p
d

Sonata in D Minor

25
mf
30
mp
cresc.
35
mf
40
cresc.
f
44
D.C.

Sonata in A Minor

K. 148
L. 64

53
mp
62
71
f
mf
80
mp
mp
88
96
e
f
g

Sonata in A Minor

15
1.
2.
mf
18
p
mf
f
21
mf
p
24
p
27
sf
p
30
mp
mf
f
1.
2.

Sonata in A Major

15
Tremulo
pp
cresc.
18
dim.
pp
20
poco a poco cresc.
22
mf
24
cresc.
mf
poco rit.

Sonata in A Major

50
mf
cresc.
58
f
p
cresc.
67
c
f
p
cresc.
76
f
mf
83
p
cresc.
89
f
1.
2.
c

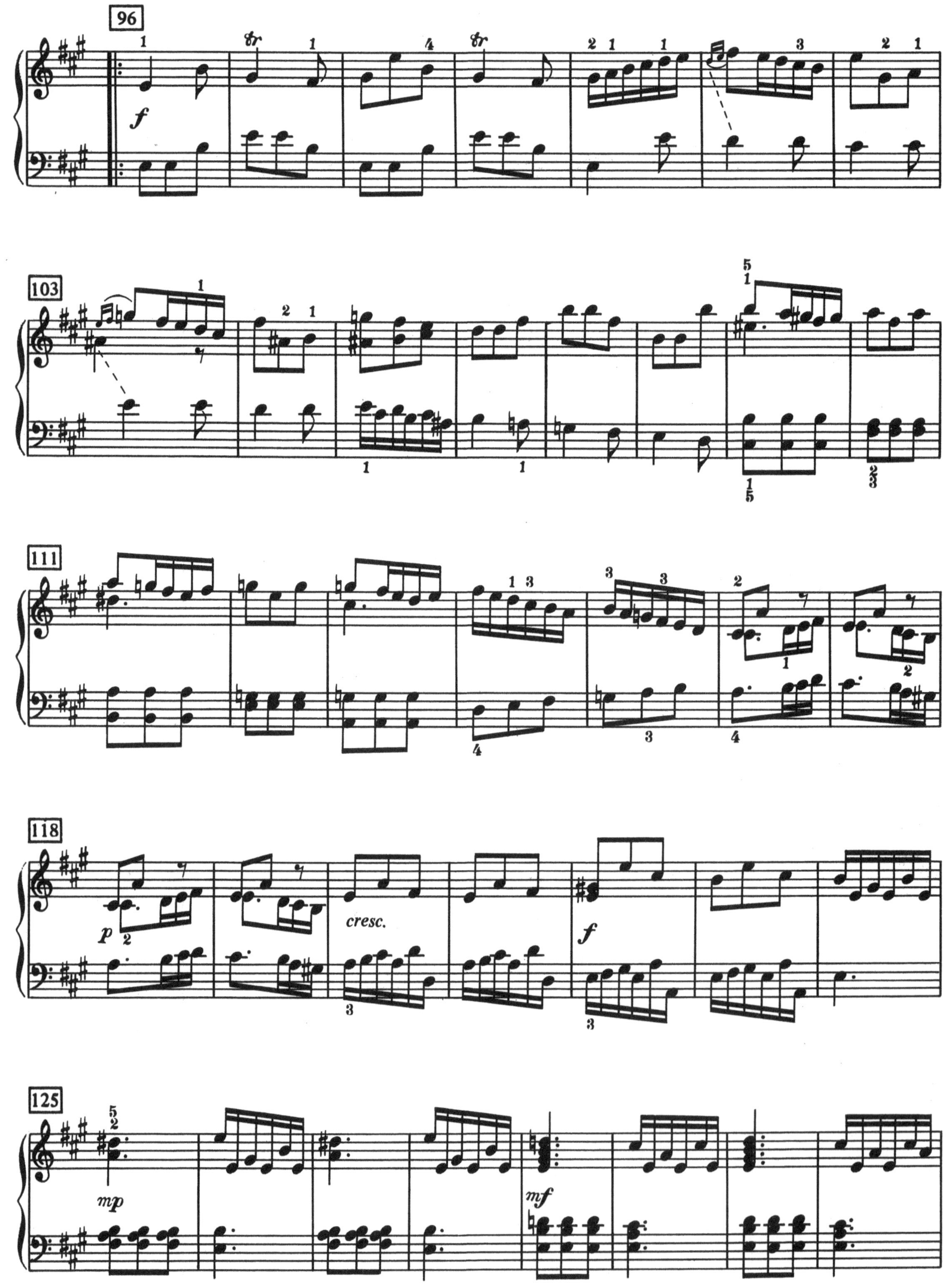
96
103
111
118
cresc.
125

133
cresc.
f
p
141
cresc.
f
p
150
cresc.
mf
f
158
p
cresc.
165
f

Sonata in F Major

24
mf
28
f
33
mp
d
tr
p cresc.
38
e
mf
p cresc.
43
mf
d
e

48

p *cresc.* *mf*

53

58

cresc. *f* *mf*

63

cresc.

67

f

Sonata in E Minor

29
mp
33
mf
c
d
tre
mp
37
tre
mf
41
tre
b
45
mp
p
cresc.
50
e
cresc.
c
d tre should be interpreted as a trill:
e A prepared trill, as in footnote a.

mf
mp
mf
mp
mf
mp
mf
poco rit.

Sonata in F Major

K. 275
L. 328

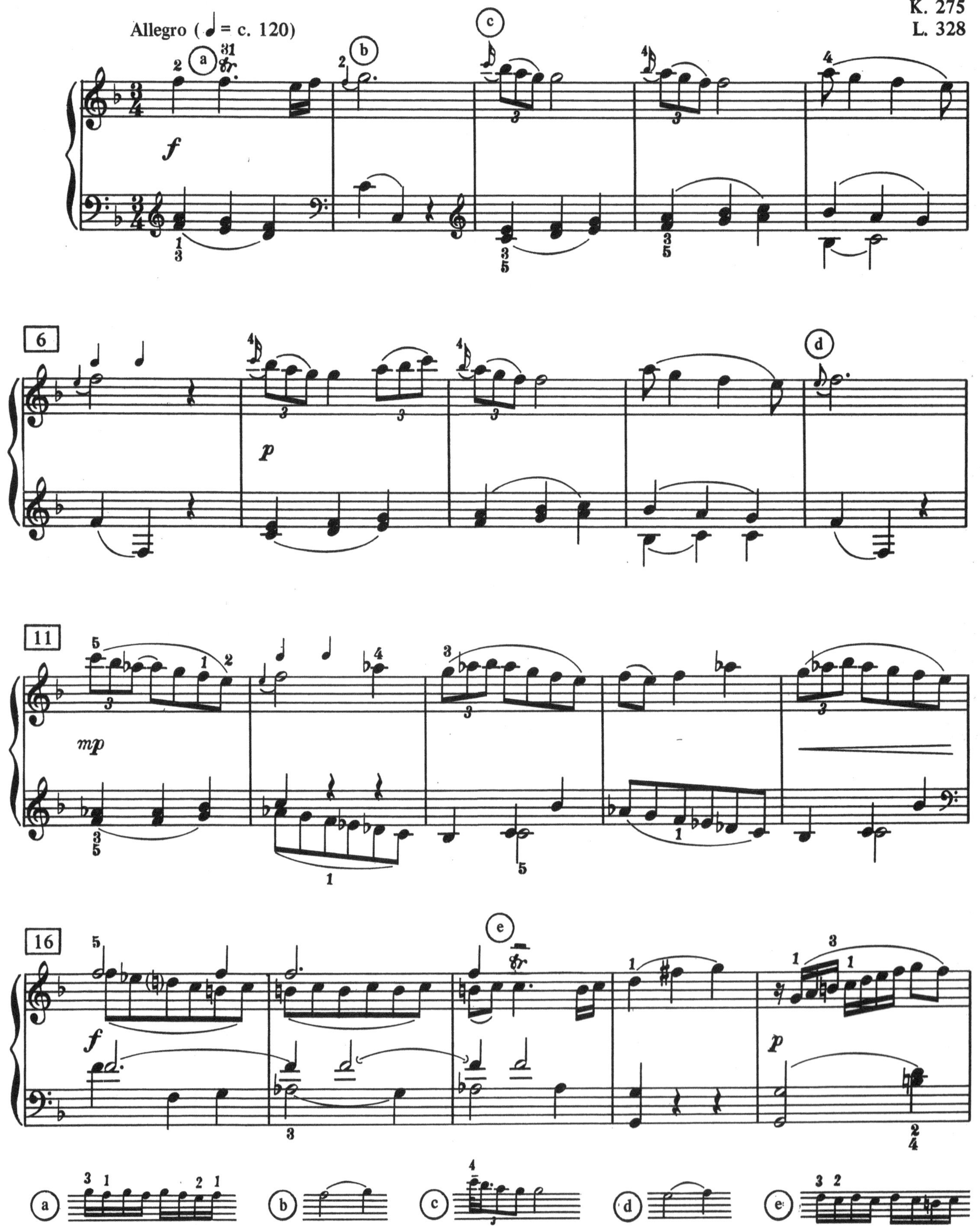

21
mp
25
f
g
p
30
g
mp
35
h
f
tr
p
h
tr
f
g
h

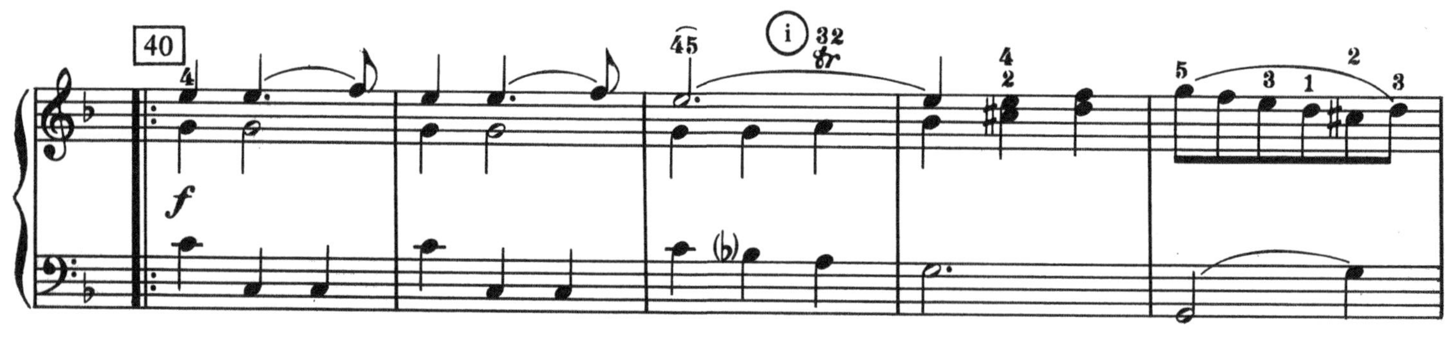
40
i
f

45
j
mp

49
f

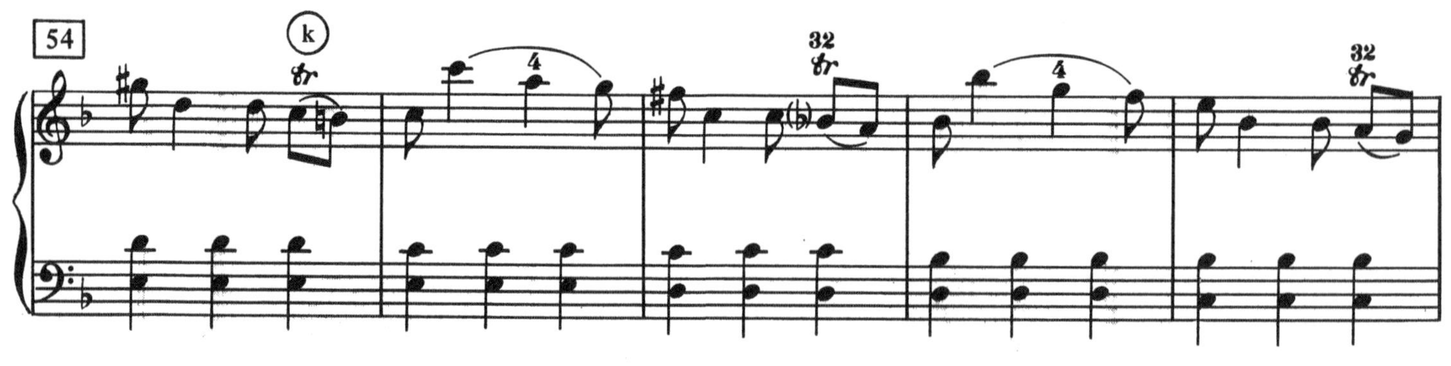
54
k

i
j
k

59
64
69
73
77
p
mp
f

Sonata in C Minor

K. 302
L. 7

20
dim.
24
mp cresc.
28
mf
32
mp
35
cresc.
38
f

42
46
49
52
56
59
p
mf
f
d
e

62
mp cresc.
66
mp cresc.
70
74
mf
78
cresc.
82
f

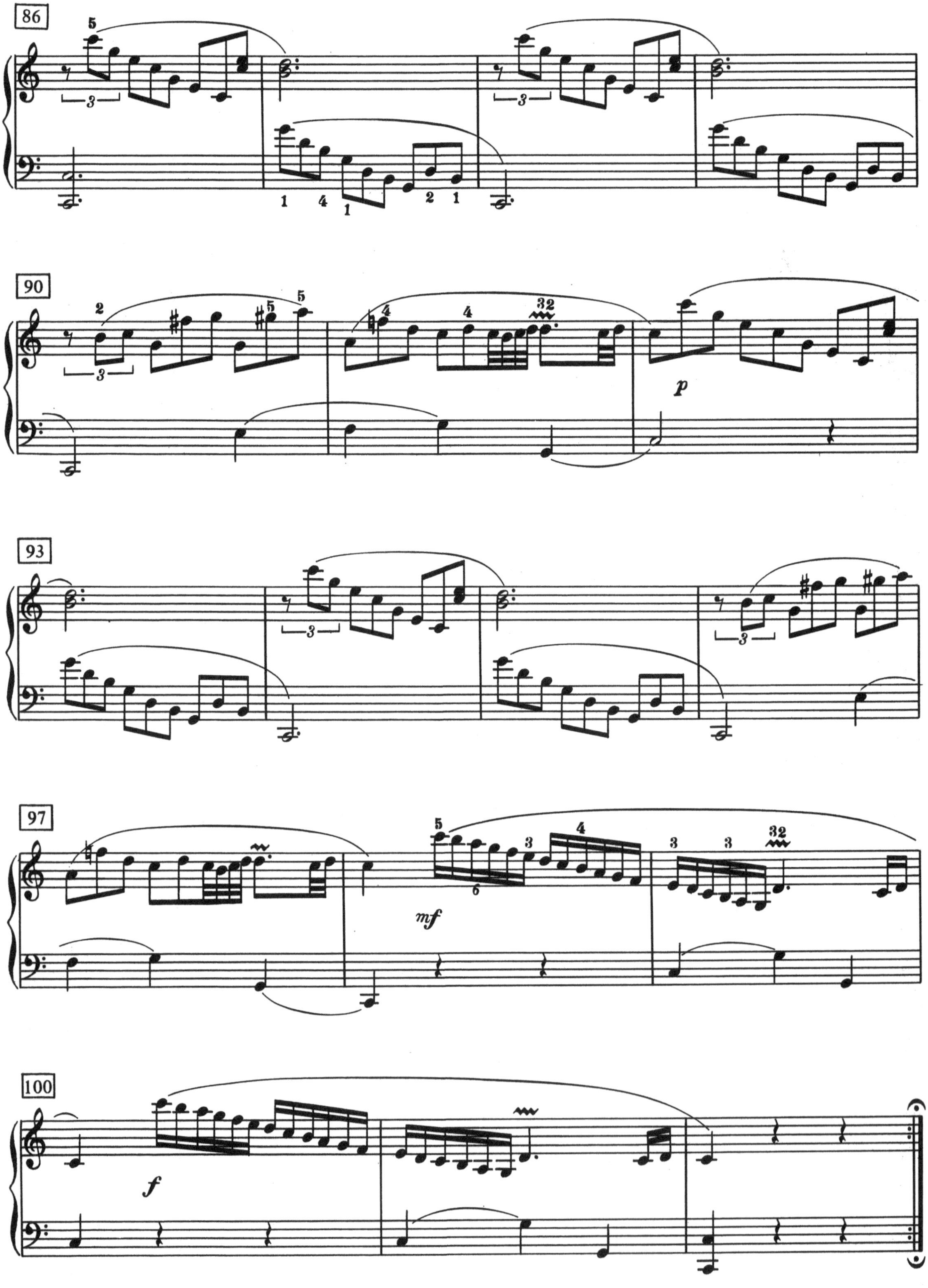

86

90

p

93

97

mf

100

f

Sonata in E Major

K. 380
L. 23

28
pp
32
c
d
p
mf
37
pp
41
mf
e
46
p
51
p
poco cresc.
più
e

55
cresc.
p mf
59
p
cresc.
mf
63
p
67
pp
71
p
mf
75
pp

Sonata in C Major

34
39
mf
44
50
mp
55
cresc.
61
f

67
75
81
87
93
99
mp
mf
cresc.
(tr)

107
mp
113
mf
119
125
mp
131
cresc.
137
f

Sonata in D Major

K. 430
L. 463

40
mp
mf
47
f
55
mp
62
cresc.
mf
68
dim.
p
cresc.

75
82
88
95
102
mp
cresc.
tr
mf
f